Colonial Park Cemetery

Savannah's Forgotten Stories

Buried America

Lexi Myers

America — Through — Time

To my husband,

You've always loved me as I am, weirdness and all.

Without your encouragement, I never would have started fully embracing all the creepy, spooky things I love. Without you, this photography doesn't happen, and these stories aren't told.

I love you forever (plus ghost time)

Fonthill Media Inc.
www.fonthillmedia.com
office@fonthillmedia.com

First published 2025

ISBN 978-1-63499-502-3

Typeset in 10pt on 13pt Sabon
Printed and bound in England

Contents

1
Welcome to Savannah

A City Built Upon Her Dead

With burials beginning in 1750, Colonial Park Cemetery is the oldest remaining cemetery in the city of Savannah, Georgia. Interments ran for over 100 years, ending in 1853 before moving to Laurel Grove Cemetery. Located in the middle of the historic district, the cemetery is a frequent stop for lovers of history and the paranormal alike; Savannah is the oldest city in Georgia and frequently at the top of "most haunted cities" lists.

While there are a few hundred headstones in the cemetery, there are estimates that put the body count near 9,000. There are a few reasons for this.

Reason 1: City Expansion: Savannah is known as "a city built upon her dead." Notice how I said that Colonial Park is the oldest standing cemetery in the city? That is because the first cemetery, located about half a mile west on Oglethorpe Avenue, was built over. While Colonial Park was left standing, it is not the full extent of its original boundaries. Abercorn Street was built in the 1890s over many of the original graves. This means that when you are driving north on that section of Abercorn Street or walking along the brick laid sidewalk on that side, you are actually walking over several hundred graves. You can see evidence of this when you are walking along this side of the cemetery as the fence is built over the top of one of the family vaults. Ghost tour guides have claimed that this is why this part of the sidewalk is so uneven as the graves are settling.

The front gate of Colonial Park Cemetery was built in 1913 and dedicated by the Daughters of the American Revolution.

Above left: This is the path just inside the main gate of the cemetery, leading to the broken graves and forgotten stories that will be covered in this book.

Above right: Azaleas and Spanish moss make Colonial Park Cemetery a classic example of a southern cemetery.

Right: The Graham Vault, located inside the gate on East Oglethorpe Avenue, was once the resting place of Revolutionary War hero Nathanael Greene. His remains were later moved to Johnson Square where there is a monument for him in the center.

Most love to visit cemeteries in the fall, but the best time to see Colonial Park is in the spring.

With the area being prone to storms, it is not uncommon to see fallen branches in the cemetery.

Empty branches stretch above the graves against the gray sky.

Colonial Park has family vaults, upright tombstones, tablets and tabletop graves throughout its acres.

Winter in the cemetery.

The original cemetery grounds extended to where the trolley is driving. Many drive and walk down Abercorn Street without realizing what (or who) they are heading over.

This vault is the final resting place of Reverend Jean Baptiste Le Moine, the first Catholic priest of Savannah who fled the French Revolution. His grave was spared during the building of the street and sidewalk, with the fence on the western side of the cemetery being built around it.

Here is another view of Reverend Le Moine's grave, with the fence built over the top, leaving the front still exposed.

The uneven sidewalk is on display after a storm with a series of puddles on the path. Rumor has it, the leveling troubles come from the graves that are settling underneath.

Reason 2: Yellow Fever: Savannah had several major yellow fever epidemics in its early history. The disease spread and killed quickly, leading to the practice of mass graves; there is one such mass grave inside of Colonial Park. Inside the East Oglethorpe Avenue entrance is a sign memorializing those lost in the epidemic of 1820. The sign reads: "Nearly 700 Savannahians died that year, including two local physicians who lost their lives caring for the stricken." Notice how it says, "nearly 700?" City legend says that the actual number was 666, but they did not want to put that number on the sign, so they rounded up.

Reason 3: Vandalism: While there is no such thing as "ok vandalism," especially when it comes to cemeteries, the vandalism of this cemetery is also historical. During the Civil War, the Union troops used this cemetery as a camp. Many graves were damaged, and some were vandalized to change the dates or ages on the headstones. The vandalized graves are still visible today and will be featured later on in this book.

One of the more unique features of this cemetery are the headstones that rest against the eastern wall. These are all headstones that belong somewhere in the cemetery; it's just that no one knows exactly where. This is due to a combination of city expansion as well as the damage from the Union troops.

The idea for this book would not have been possible without coming across the grave of Isabella Chadbourn. Her grave caught my eye back in 2020 as I was walking around the cemetery. I felt drawn to hers in particular because I noticed the break at the bottom; when I saw she was only twenty-one years old, my heart broke. A few years later, seeing her again, I decided to look her up on findagrave.com to see what I could learn about her. Her notes included that she died from poisoning by oil. This started a massive search of her and her family tree to see what I could learn about her.

Inside the gate on Oglethorpe Avenue sits this sign that is dedicated to victims of the 1820 yellow fever epidemic. Two of the town's doctors died during the epidemic, along with hundreds of others. While the sign says, "nearly 700," rumor says it was actually 666 victims.

Misplaced and broken tombstones line the eastern wall of the cemetery. This is due to vandalism as well as expansion.

Some sections of the wall have multiple rows of broken tombstones. These people may not have known each other in life or even be buried near each other, but they now have this place in common.

Isabella was born on November 26, 1808, to Charles and Sophia Gildon; she was one of six children, with an older half-sister, an older sister and brother, and a younger sister and brother. Her paternal grandmother's name was Isabel, so it seems she was named after her.

She married Henry Champion on November 14, 1824, just shy of her sixteenth birthday. They had two children together: Isabella Sophia in 1825 and Henry Jr. in 1826. Sadly, Isabella Sophia would pass away September 16, 1826. The family was living in Massachusetts at the time, leaving her to be buried there.

The year 1827 would not be much better for Isabella. Her husband died on September 3. Three days later, her mother would pass away as well; both died from fever. Her family tree stories state that her second husband, Jacob Chadbourn, was helping her manage Henry's estate when they "became close." They married on September 22, 1828, when she was twenty years old. Not only was she married again, but she became a stepmother. Jacob had a daughter, Sarah, from his first marriage. Jacob was quite a bit older than Isabella, though; he was forty-two when they were wed. His daughter, Sarah, was the same age as Isabella. This did not seem to affect the relationship between the two women, though, as Sarah would eventually name her own daughter, Isabelle, after marrying Isabella's brother-in-law from her first marriage, John.

Isabella died on June 19, 1830; records show she died from an overdose of oil of tansy. Oil of tansy was commonly used at that time to treat menstrual cramps. Her grave, though broken, once read: "She was the most affectionate and best of wives."

Her son, Henry Jr., was taken from his stepfather and put into the care of Aaron and Mary Jane Champion. Mary Jane was Isabella's older half-sister, and she married Aaron Champion, who was Henry Sr.'s older brother. You can tour Aaron Champion's former home today, the historic Harper Fowlkes House on Orleans Square. Henry Jr. would die tragically young, passing away from fever when he was eighteen years old. He never had any children, so Isabella's direct family line ended there. With no one to visit Isabella anymore, I felt even more drawn to visit her and have been doing so frequently since learning her story.

Throughout this book, I hope to share more stories of people like Isabella, graves that are frequently passed by without their lives ever being known.

I left these flowers at the grave of Isabella Chadbourn in November 2023 in honor of her birthday. When I got there with my flowers, I saw someone had already left her a rose made from a palm leaf. It seems her story is spreading, which is what I want for her and others shared in this book; no one's story should ever be forgotten.

Flowers were left by someone unknown at this grave in the northern end of the cemetery.

2
Cemetery Vandalism

Historic Graffiti

As I have previously mentioned, the cemetery is home to a number of vandalized graves, with vandalism dating back to the 1800s. Throughout my visits to the cemetery, I have come across three different graves with their ages altered; I found a fourth in my photographs while doing research.

The first grave is that of Christopher McDonald. No one knows exactly where in the cemetery he is buried because his tombstone rests against the east wall of the cemetery with the other displaced stones. His tombstone reads: "Sacred to the memory of Christopher McDonald who died 1st March 1844 aged 42 years. May his soul rest in peace. Amen. This stone is erected by his widow." His age has been changed on the stone to say he lived to be 421 years old.

Christopher was born in Ireland in 1802, coming to America by way of Charleston, South Carolina, in August 1822. He became a citizen on January 30, 1832, while living in Georgia. On April 22, 1837, he married another Irish immigrant, Ellenor Sullivan, at Saint John's in Savannah. They had three children together: James William in 1838, Ellenora in 1841, and Jane Ann in 1842. Sadly, little Ellenora would pass away in September 1842 from inflammatory bowels; she was only ten months old. Christopher would die two years later, on March 4, 1844, from consumption.

The next vandalized grave I noticed was the Morecock-Woolhopter family grave. This grave covers four individuals: Catharine Morecock, Phillip Woolhopter, Sarah Ann Woolhopter, and Elizabeth M. Woolhopter. The inscription reads: "Underneath this marble are deposited the remains of Catharine Morecock, who died 15th Feb 1815 aged 69 years and 5 months and Phillip D. Woolhopter who died 11th Feb 1818, aged 49 years. Also his two infant children, Sarah Ann Woolhopter who died 1810 aged 10 months and 27 days. And Elizabeth M. Woolhopter, who died 1813 aged 14 months." Two of the ages are vandalized here; Phillip is shown to be 1,491 years old, while Sarah Ann is shown to have lived to ten months and 1,271 days.

Catharine was born in South Carolina in 1743, marrying Samuel Morecock in 1766. They had six children together. Their youngest daughter, Sarah, married

Christopher McDonald's grave is meant to read, "Sacred to the memory of Christopher McDonald who died 1st March 1844 aged 42 years. May his soul rest in peace, amen. This stone is erected by his widow."

A close-up shows where vandals added a "1" to make his age "421 years."

Christopher's tombstone is one of the largest on the eastern wall, sitting in the far left of this photo.

The Woolhopter family grave has two ages that have had extra "1s" added to it. Father, Phillip, was changed to be 1,491 years old, while daughter, Sarah Ann, was changed to be ten months and 1,271 days (which all together would be about four years old).

Phillip Woolhopter in Savannah on February 1, 1804. Born in New York to German immigrants in 1769, Phillip was a publisher. Sarah and Phillip would have three children together: Phillip Jr. in 1808, Sarah Ann in 1810, and Elizabeth in 1811. We know, sadly, that only Phillip Jr. would live to adulthood. Both Sarah Ann and Elizabeth are noted as dying from "teething," in 1810 and 1813 respectively. Catharine died from pleurisy on February 13, 1813. Phillip's records just show that he "declined" in health, passing away on February 11, 1818. Their remains are here while Sarah and Phillip Jr. are buried in Laurel Grove.

While I found the previously mentioned graves a few years ago, I recently saw the grave of Wesley Abbott. Like Christopher, we do not know exactly where he is buried because his stone is located along the eastern cemetery wall. The inscription is hard to read, but it does show that his age was changed to be 541 years old.

Wesley, a silversmith, was born in 1801. He married Ophelia Lightbourn on Christmas Eve in 1839. Ophelia had a son, Samuel, from a previous marriage who would have been nine years old at the time. Wesley passed away three years later on October 31, 1842.

Above left: Wesley Abbott's tombstone is nearly illegible. It is meant to read, "In memory of Wesley Abbott a native of New Jersey but for the last sixteen years a resident of this city who departed this life on the 31st October 1842, aged 44 years."

Above right: Closer inspection of the tombstone shows where they added a "5" to make him "544 years old." Like Christopher McDonald, his grave is both vandalized and lost.

His cause of death is listed as being marasmus, which is severe malnutrition. It seems unlikely that he would have starved to death while the rest of the family was well; Ophelia would go on to live for another twelve years while Samuel lived until 1872. Certain infections can lead to marasmus, though, by first causing chronic diarrhea. In any case, poor Wesley had a painful end and now rests in an unmarked grave; the marker he once had has been vandalized.

While researching and looking at photographs, I found the grave of Captain Jonathan Cooper to be vandalized as well. I discovered this while researching the grave of his wife and son, Julia Ann and William, who I will be covering later on. Jonathan lived to be seventy years old, but his grave was altered to say 1,700 years old. His grave was meant to read: "In memory of Capt. Jonathan Cooper, Born in Wexford, Ireland, but for a number of years a resident of this place who died on 13th March 1838; aged 70 years. Here lies the best of fathers, a sincere friend, an honest man." He was a harbor master at the time of his death from "apoplexy," which is a bleed in the brain. He is buried next to his wife and son, having never appeared to remarry after Julia's death in 1813.

Captain Jonathan Cooper is the oldest man in the cemetery at "1700" years old, thanks to vandals. He died when he was seventy from apoplexy, which is a brain bleed.

3

The Eastern Wall

Missing Pieces

The lone wall of the cemetery sits on the eastern edge, running between the cemetery and the police station. Some stones were broken during the Civil War, while others were displaced due to city expansion. Knocked over, crumbling, or otherwise damaged, they have found their way back here for preservation while the actual gravesite is still unknown.

While their stories are all different, these people have one tragic ending in common: their graves have been left unmarked for all time. Their descendants would have no way of knowing where they are buried, just that their remains are somewhere in the 6-acre cemetery.

This "feature" of the cemetery is often pointed out on tours and is frequently visited. While there are many visitors to this section of the cemetery, many are unaware of the stories of the people whose graves were disturbed.

Sarah Hill-Norris has one of the longest epitaphs I have ever seen. It reads:

> Sacred to the memory of Sarah Hill, wife of James Norris, who departed this life on the 26th day of June 1835 in the 30th year of her age. Beneath this monument repose her mortal remains beside those of her two infant children, the younger of whom Thomas Benjamin who lived but a day after his birth. Of the deceased mother it is recorded with truth that in her were combined render union happy, life endearing virtue, amiable and religion admired and esteemed. Patiently did she suffer and calmly did she recline her head on the pillow of affliction whilst she yielded immortal spirit into the hands of her Creator, in the full hope of a glorious resurrection, in her death was exemplified the truth which the following effusion records. Sweet is the scene when virtue dies, when sinks a righteous soul to rest, how mildly beam the closing eye, how gently heaves the expiring breast. A holy quiet reins around, a calm which nothing can destroy, naught can disturb that peace profound which their unfettered souls enjoy. Its duty done as sinks the day, light from its load, the spirit flies while heaven and earth combined to say, sweet is the scene when virtue dies.

John J. Evans was born in South Carolina in 1783 and was a printer by trade. He had been living in Savannah for about five years at the time of his passing on January 15, 1813, from convulsions at age thirty. Death records show that he was married and he had a sister, but their names were not available.

"Erected by Mich. O'Connor in memory of his wife Alice." Alice was born in Ireland but was a resident of Savannah when she died at age thirty-eight from fever in October 1821.

She was married to James Norris, and they had four children, though only one would live to adulthood. Two of the infants were buried with her somewhere in this cemetery.

Henrietta Burk was born in 1797 and was first married to a man named James Jackson. Henrietta and James had three children together: Drucilla in 1814, Eliza in 1816, and Abraham in 1818. James passed away in 1823; Henrietta married Major Howell Burk on February 16, 1824. Her death records show that she died of brain inflammation in 1830.

Moses Warner was born in Massachusetts on December 22, 1792, to Joseph and Jerusha Warner. He was one of eleven children and had a twin sister, Miriam. Sadly, Miriam died a few months shy of their second birthday. He was a merchant by trade, passing away in Savannah from consumption a few days after his twenty-seventh birthday in 1819.

It would seem that Patrick O'Byrne was traveling in Savannah from Ireland when he died as he is listed as being a non-resident on his death records; he died of fever when he was thirty-eight years old. His epitaph says that his tombstone was erected (meaning paid for) by his brother, Edward. It seems entirely likely that it was cheaper and easier at the time to pay for a grave than it would have been to transport a body home.

Back in the 1800s, it was common to end up in prison for not paying debts. This seems to be the case for Mr. Noah Bradley as the only records that exist for him are court records that list him as being a debtor. It would not be out of the realm of possibility that he died in prison as prisons in the nineteenth century were not always clean and safe. This is, however, impossible to confirm without proper records.

Mary Ginovoly has one of the wildest epitaphs I have ever read. It is inscribed:

> To the memory of Mary Ginovoly who departed this life the 5th of December 1812 Aged 61 years. I know that my Redeemer liveth, and that he will stand at the latter day upon the Earth; and though after my death worms destroy this body, yet in my flesh shall I see God; whom I shall see for myself, and mine eyes shall behold, and not another. Jesus said unto her, I am the Resurrection and the Life; He that believeth in me, though he were dead yet shall he live.

Mary was born in South Carolina in 1751 and died in Savannah on December 5, 1812, when she was sixty-one years old.

Shapleigh Ricker was born in New Hampshire on August 6, 1790, and he would pass away in Savannah from fever when he was only twenty-nine years old. His inscription reads:

> Erected to the memory of Shapleigh Ricker, A native of Portsmouth, New Hampshire, who died August 15th, 1819 aged 29 years and 9 days. He left a widow and one child to bemoan their loss. Lord I commit my soul to thee, accept the sacred trust; receive this nobler part of me, and watch my sleeping dust.

David Frink Jr. was born in the 1790s in New London, CT, to David and Desire Frink. Some records have him being born in 1791 while others have 1794. They may have gotten his date of birth wrong or his age wrong; without the records of his death, we

Right: Sarah Hill-Norris died after a long illness, with her death records showing she died from "bilious fever." This is a fever associated with liver dysfunction and was often caused by malaria during those times.

Below left: Henrietta Burk's epitaph was meant to read, "Mrs. Henrietta Burk, wife of Howell D. Burk … Waynesboro, GA. Died April 26, 1830, aged 33 years."

Below right: James Dunn was from New Jersey, a mason by trade, and died from consumption in March 1822 when he was twenty-seven years old. His epitaph reads, "Erected to the memory of James Dunn, a native of New Jersey and a respectable resident …"

"In memory of Moses Warner of Pittsfield, Mass., son of Joseph Warner of Northampton, Mass. who died in this place December 27, 1819, aged 27 years."

Joseph Warner's headstone rests next to a broken, nameless stone.

"Sacred to the memory of John Eagerty a native of the County of Kerry Ireland who departed this life on the 5th day of December 1845 aged 26 years ... youth he was religious ... and industrious and one of ... class who create no enemies nor ever lose a friend. Requiescat in pace."

"Sacred to the memory of Patrick O'Byrne who departed this life 10th July 1830 in the 38th year of his age. Requiescat in pace. A native of Kiltemaugh, County of Mayo, Ireland. This monument is erected by his brother Edward O'Byrne."

Left: "Noah Bradley, A Native of Greenfield, Connec … Feb 1776 … 1811."

Below left: Older epitaphs give a lot more detail than they do today and, in some cases, can be more graphic. Mary Ginovoly's epitaph goes so far as to mention worms destroying her body after death.

Below right: There is not much information available about Shapleigh or his family, but we know he was married and had one child.

cannot know for sure. The only record of what happened to him is on this tombstone, showing that he drowned in the Savannah River. Family trees have him being the second youngest of eight children, with three sisters and four brothers.

Samuel and Carolina Modrdecai wed on November 12, 1809. They had a son, David, in 1812 and a daughter, Matilda, in April 1817.

September 1819 was a tragic month for the Mordecai family as they lost their two children only weeks apart. Matilda was only two years old when she died on September 11; David was not much older at seven on September 29. Matilda's cause of death is listed as being "mortification," which at the time typically meant gangrene. David's cause of death is listed as being "worms."

Samuel and Carolina would go on to have three more children after the deaths of David and Matilda; James in 1820, Abraham in 1825, and Georgia in 1829. Sadly, they would never get to meet their older siblings and today we do not know where they are buried.

You may recognize the name Sophia Gildon from earlier in this book; Sophia is the mother of Isabella Chadbourn.

Sophia was born on January 4, 1783, in New Canaan, CT, to parents Frederick and Ester Selleck. She was married sometime in 1800 to Richard Griggs, and they had a daughter in 1802 named Mary Jane. Sadly, Richard would pass away that same year. In 1803, she married Charles Gildon, and they would have five children together; their

Above left: "In memory of David Frink Junior, aged 25 years, son of David and Dezire Frink of New London, Connect. He drowned in the Savannah River."

Above right: David Frink's footstone rests a few stones down from his headstone.

"Sacred to the memory of Matilda Mordecai Daughter of Samuel and Carolina Mordecai who died Sept … 18…. Also their son, David M. Mordecai who died Sept 29, 1819."

"In memory of Sarah Antoinette Dayton who died October 9, 1821 aged 2 years." Sarah Antoinette was born in Boston in 1819. At some point her family relocated to Savannah as she is listed as a resident at the time of her death. She died from "fever" in October 1821.

Sarah Dayton's tombstone rests next to the stone of the Mordecai siblings.

oldest son was named Richard. At first glance that may look like it was for her first husband, but Charles's father was named Richard as well.

Sophia died on September 6, 1827, from "fever." Newspapers at that time described her death as being from "a short but painful illness."

Eliza Croker (spelled on her death record as Kroker) was born in Florida in 1817. She and George were married on June 13, 1839. Their married life would be cut short as Eliza died from childbirth on July 3, 1840. The child did not survive and was buried with their mother.

There was a little bit of confusion when I was researching the Williams family. The epitaph says that Feriby died on October 13, 1804. There are no death records for her on that date, but there is one for November 1. I am inclined to think that it is her, because I cannot imagine that there are many Feriby (also spelled Ferreby) Williamses that are married to men named John that died in Savannah in 1804. Per that record, she died of consumption. Sadly, there are not any records for the death of their daughter, Louisa, and it is unknown right now if they had any other children.

Abigail Lillibridge was born in 1759 in Newport, RI. She and her husband, John, had five sons together: Oliver, Hampton, Gardner (Abigail's maiden name), Robert, and the unnamed infant that we can assume she died giving birth to.

"In memory of Sophia, wife of Charles Gildon Esq. A native of New Canaan, Conn. Died Sept. 5th 1827 aged 41 years and 9 months." Sophia is the mother of Isabella. Though Sophia's grave is unmarked, I hope they are buried near each other.

"Sacred to the memory of Mrs. Eliza, wife of George Croker who died July 3rd, 1840 aged 23 years. Also her infant babe. A native of Amelia Island, East Florida. As she lived, she died, in grace with God and her neighbor. May she rest in peace. Amen."

"In memory of Feriby Williams, wife of John Williams who departed this life October 13, 1804 aged 30 years. Grace was in all her steps, Heaven in her eyes … gesture, dignity and love. Also Louisa B. Williams, their daughter who departed this life June 13, 1800 aged 4 years and 3 months."

"In memory of Mrs. Abigail Lillibridge, wife of Mr. John Lillibridge of Newport, Rho. & her infant son who departed this life the 3rd Dec. 1796 in the 37th year of her age."

"In memory of Joseph S. Warner of Providence, RI who died August 27, 1813 in the 21st year of his age. Amiable in his disposition and loved and respected by all who knew him, remarkable for his integrity as a merchant…" Joseph Warner was born in 1792 in Providence, RI; he died in Savannah at age twenty-one from "fever" on August 27, 1813.

"In memory of Levi Wrist who died Feb. 23, 1819 in the 35 year of his age." Levi was a carpenter; his cause of death does not appear to be given. Usually, the death records will have "ditto" marks if they died from the same cause as the person listed before them, but his does not even have that.

Josiah Muir was born in New Jersey on July 6, 1780. Mary was born Mary Tucker, and she was born in 1776 in New York. They were married on November 17, 1803, and they had three children together: Aurelia, Lewis, and Louisa. October 1820 was a terrible month for the family. Josiah died on the 1st, while Lewis died on the 18th. They are both noted as dying of "fever," and given the yellow fever outbreak of 1820, it feels safe to assume that is what killed them. It would not be long until Mary died, also succumbing to "fever" on August 25, 1823. Aurelia would have been eighteen at this time, so it is likely that she took over the care of her younger sister, Louisa.

Above left: "In memory of Josiah Muir who departed this life Oct. 1st, 1820 aged 41 years & Mary his wife who died Aug 25th 1823 aged 47 years Also Lewis Phoenix their son who died Oct 18 1820 aged 12 years."

Above right: This row of the wall has Patrick O'Byrne's stone along with Anna Mary and two others that are harder to read.

David Frink's headstone rests at the end of this row. Underneath these headstones is resurrection fern; it is typically dried up, coming back to life briefly after it rains.

Joseph Warner's headstone rests here in the middle.

This section with the double row contains many of those we have talked about in this chapter: Abigail Lillibridge, the Muir family, Feriby and Louisa Williams, and Henrietta Burk.

Mary Ginovoly's tombstone rests here with the Long siblings and Robert Christie. No death records exist for Michael Long but his older sister, Eliza Keen, died from dropsy (swelling from heart failure) when she was forty-eight. Robert Christie was a clerk who died from consumption on Christmas Eve 1822 when he was thirty-five.

These tombstones belong to Thomas Mazcyk and Jane Carnochan. Thomas Winstanly Mazcyk was from Charleston and died of yellow fever when he was only fifteen in 1827. Little Jane died when she was only seven from fever and a bowel obstruction in 1825.

To the left is the tombstone of the Taylor siblings, Samuel and Catherine. Samuel died in 1830 when he was only fifteen months old; Catherine died eight months later in 1831 when she was five years old. Samuel died of croup and Catherine died from dropsy.

To the left of John Evans's tombstone is Hampton Baxter Lillibridge's tombstone. He died in 1817 at age twenty-five from what's only explained as inflammation.

These are the tombstones of Mary Jane Green and Lewis Hayt. Lewis, a clerk from Boston, died in 1823 when he was twenty-nine years old from fever. Mary Jane died at twenty in 1840 from inflammatory bowels.

Behind this wall you can see the police station. Life continues busily outside of the cemetery's barriers.

Spring is always the most beautiful time in the cemetery while the azaleas are in full bloom.

The eastern wall rests in the shade of ancient trees.

These headstones belong to John Davidson (age thirty-nine), William Coe (age thirty-five), Richard E. W. Craven (age seventeen), and George Walter (age twenty-five). Not all death records are available, but William died from convulsions and Richard died by drowning.

4
Yellow Fever

Epidemic Disasters

Savannah has had several yellow fever epidemics throughout its history, with the disease taking hold of the city in 1733, 1820, and 1876. The worst outbreak came in 1820, with almost 700 lives being lost. Many were buried in unmarked graves from the start as there was a mass grave for those who died from the disease. There is a plaque inside one of the gates to memorialize those who were lost.

As I was going through death records for others, I saw in the 1820 pages there was row after row listing "fever" as the cause of death; sometimes it would be the entire page. I selected a few names from that year and looked into their story for the captions of this chapter. It should be noted that these photos are scenes from the cemetery and give no indication to the actual location of the mass grave as its exact location is not known.

Valentine Torretton died at twenty-nine years old on July 9, 1820, from fever. He was a carpenter from Ireland.

Abel Gibson died on July 22, 1820, from fever when he was thirty-five. He was also a carpenter, though he was from Massachusetts.

The couple Philip and Philiphina Box are buried somewhere in this cemetery. They were married on March 23, 1810, when she was twenty-four and he was thirty-seven; they did not appear to have any children. They both died from fever on August 7, 1820.

Ann Downing was born in Ireland in 1803, dying of fever in Savannah when she was seventeen on September 9, 1820.

Bastian Levy died on August 17, 1820, when he was twenty-seven years old; no occupational records exist for him, but he was born in Spain.

Daniel Quilliam was from England, dying from fever in Savannah on August 17, 1820, as well.

L. P. Johnston was from Savannah; he was born in 1797 and died from fever on September 11, 1820, when he was twenty-three years old. We cannot tell what L. P. stood for based on the records, but we do know he was an accountant.

Much like L. P., we do not know what the "J." in J. Scozbery stands for. We do know he was from Holland, was a seaman, and died on September 12, 1820, when he was fifty from fever.

Somewhere in this cemetery lies the Foster brothers, Charles and Harrison, who died one day apart in September 1820 from fever. Charles was a thirty-year-old grocer and Harrison was a twenty-three-year-old bar keeper. While there is no tombstone for them here, their family placed one in their native Massachusetts for them.

Rose Reily was thirty when she died on September 20, 1820. She was a servant from Ireland. Her death records specify she had "black vomit," which is characteristic of yellow fever as sufferers often vomit blood.

Henry McCoy was the constable, dying at age sixty on September 21, 1820.

Sadly, there are many listed with "name unknown" in the healthcare records, so even their general whereabouts were not known by their families.

Right: Euxlio Delgado was a soldier from Spain who died from fever. He was only thirty-six when he died on September 6, 1820.

Below left: Amidee Godefroy died at age twenty-four on September 29, 1820, from fever. They were a clerk originally from France.

Below right: Sadly, like the Foster brothers, the Snider sisters are buried somewhere in this cemetery in unmarked graves. Katherine was born in 1810, and Abigail was born in 1813. Both died in September 1820 from fever; Abigail died on the 28th and Katherine died on the 30th.

5

Broken or Nearly Illegible

Finding Lost Names

Broken and crumbling graves are a common sight in a cemetery this old, though it is still heart-breaking to see. It is hard to imagine burying someone you love just for their name to be lost to time. The following graves with names nearly lost or broken were naturally harder to research, but it was worth the effort to keep their names alive.

Joanna Clark's cause of death is listed as being from "decay of liver," which gives evidence to the long affliction noted in her epitaph. She was born in New Jersey in 1761, and she was married to James Clark. There are two different James Clarks from Savannah that would potentially fit: Captain James Clark from New York who died in Savannah from consumption in 1819 when he was fifty-nine; or James Clark from Scotland who died from inflammatory bowels in 1820 when he was sixty-eight. I lean towards the first James Clark because he would have been closer in age to Joanna, and he was also from the northeast.

There was not much to be found about this broken grave in terms of family members. William C. Mills would have been born about 1790 based on his age at time of death and is listed as being a native of Georgia and resident of Savannah. His cause of death is listed as being "intemperance," meaning he was an alcoholic. Whether he drank himself to death one night or he died from something long term like cirrhosis of the liver is impossible to say, though jaundice is sometimes noted in the death records if it occurs.

One of the more frustrating things to come across in a cemetery is a grave that does not have the person's complete name on it. Unfortunately, I have seen it happen a lot to women where their graves are simply carved with "Wife of" and their husband's name without any mention of theirs. In the case of A. Sherlock, they did not include her husband's full name either, which made researching her a little harder.

In the southwestern corner of the cemetery, alone at the end of the path, is the grave of Ann Sherlock. She was born in Balbriggan, Ireland, in 1799. At some point, she came to America; she was married to J. Sherlock, though we are not sure when. She died on February 3, 1822, from consumption. Ann's grave has started to crumble at the top and also appears to be sinking as the bottom half of her epitaph cannot be read.

"Sacred to the memory of Hiram LeForce who died Oct 26, 1817 aged 12 years." Poor Hiram died young, and his stone is broken to where many would not be able to find out what his name was. You can faintly see "LeForce" and twelve years. There is, sadly, no other information available for him.

This grave is broken to the point of beginning to open.

This broken and faded grave sadly rests on the ground.

Some graves are protected by fences and gates, though that does not stop them from fading.

"In memory of Joanna Clark, wife of James Clark, who departed this life Novr 27 1808, aged 47 years. Afflictions sore long time she bore, physicians' aid was vain, till God did please give her ease and free her from her pain." This is what her stone is meant to read as all that is currently legible is "Joanna" and "47." Many of these graves were pieced together with an interment list.

Sadly, this grave is too worn to see who it belongs to.

The only thing legible on this broken, faded tomb is "aged 10 years."

"George W., son of John D. & EA Mallette, died 22nd March 1847 aged 6 months and 22 days. Of such is the kingdom of God."

This is either a broken grave or a remnant of a footstone, but either way it gives no identification to the two-year-old that is buried here.

"In memory of John Drinker Fisher, the son of Hendrich & Deborah Fisher, who departed this life the 27th day of December 1793, aged 4 years, 2 months and 20 days. Think mighty God on feeble man how few his hours and short his span short from the cradle to the grave." His stone is discolored and beginning to crumble on the top edge.

While there is not much left of this stone at all, someone did stop to leave something for this unknown person; you can see the drink umbrella sitting just in front of it.

"Sacred to the memory of William Taylor, a native of Castelcomer, County of Kilkenny, Ireland, who departed this life June 5th 1831 aged 35 years." William Taylor was born in Ireland around 1796. It is unknown when he came to Savannah, but he is listed as being a shopkeeper at the time of his death from consumption.

"... ory of William C. Mills, who departed this life Nov 6th 1827, aged 37 years."

Above left: "Sacred to the memory of A. Sherlock, consort of J. Sherlock, who departed this life Jan. 31 1822 age 22 years. A native of Balbriggan, County Dublin, Ireland."

Above right: This is another angle of Ann Sherlock's grave, showing how much further back it is located. It sits in the back corner of the cemetery next to a bench, away from other graves.

Left: This faded and crumbling grave rests a few steps behind the grave of Ann Sherlock.

The grave next to Isabella from the beginning of this book is that of Thomas Price, which appears to have been broken in half and then repaired. Thomas was born in New Jersey, but later became a resident of Savannah. According to records, he was a merchant; he died of "fits," likely meaning some kind of seizure.

Is there a more beautiful name than Serene Wise? Little Serene was born to Stephen and an unknown mother (her name is not on Serene's death record) in February 1803. She had a short life, dying of convulsions on October 24, 1807; her death record notes it as being "very sudden." Stephen, a bricklayer, would die three years later, also from convulsions. His grave is unmarked in Colonial Park, but I am hoping that it is near hers. Her grave is showing some of the discoloration similar to John Drinker Fisher.

"Sacred to the memory of Thomas R. Price, a native of Newark, N. Jersey who died Feby. 22, 1827 in the 35th year of his age."

"In memory of Serene Wise, who departed this life on the 24th of October 1807, aged 3 years and 8 months. Beloved parents weep not for my fate, my soul's exalted to a blissful state ... meet again when earths pursuits ... endless bliss and there to part no more."

These graves are being taken over by nature, with the roots of an oak tree growing around them. They have almost nearly consumed the one.

This is a close-up of the grave that is surrounded by tree roots. Sadly, the name and epitaph are too faded.

"In memory of Amie Arnold, died April 1872 aged 78 years. I long to see the season come when children come home to God … Mother of Harry Bla."

"Charlotte, wife of John E. Rowson and daughter of the Rev. John Beverly of Kingstown Upon Hull England. Obt. Sep. 20 1818 age 46. Wher's the lyre that often spoke and the heart's affection told; friends beloved the lyre is broke the sympathizing heart is cold."

Not a lot of information is given here, making me believe this is Robert Mitchell's footstone. He was born in 1776 and died in December 1830.

6

A Different Time

Stories of Loss

While no family is without its troubles, families in the seventeenth and eighteenth centuries suffered in ways that we cannot quite picture today. Disease ran rampant, many died young, parents often outlived their children, and mothers died before getting to meet the babies that they carried for nine months. These tragedies are just a few of what I encountered while researching this cemetery.

Bridget Royston was born in Ireland in 1782. Her death records are extremely detailed. She died from a "disorder on the lungs—consumption." The notes read, "Sick 10 weeks, during which time she was unable to turn herself from bed. Died childless."

Not much outside of what is mentioned on the tombstone can be found about Dr. Samuel Vickers. TL was his younger brother, and he was buried in New Jersey. Their mother, Sarah, sadly outlived them both.

> Sacred to the memory of Rosannah Millen, wife of John Millen, who departed this life 20th Feby 1810 in the 58th year of her age. The just is blessed she lived by faith, she slept in Jesus and shall awake with joy at the resurrection of the just to inherit eternal glory. This stone tells where reposes the remains of John Millen who departed this life 28th Oct 1811 aged 54 years. The following lines are expressive of his sufferings and expectations. Afflictions weight I long had borne and tried the healing art in vain till mercy whispered cease to mourn and death released me from my pain. Death came by sin but even death is made away from pain through Christ our living head.

Julia Ann would have been born about 1788 based on her age at her time of death. She was married to Captain Jonathan Cooper, and they had one child together, William, born in September 1811. The year 1813 would be life altering for Captain Cooper. First, William died in April from "teething." Julia Ann would then die in November from "inflammation of the brain." It does not appear that Jonathan ever remarried, passing away over twenty years later in 1838; he is buried next to his wife and child. His grave was previously featured as one of the vandalized graves.

"Sacred to the memory of Mrs. Bridget Royston, consort of Capt. Wm Royston, who departed this life on the 28th day of October 1806. Aged 24 years. She was a native of Carrickonsuir, Ireland who lived beloved and died lamented by all that knew her. May she rest in peace. Amen."

"Here lies interred the body of Doctor Samuel Vickers, who departed this life Octor the 15th anno domini 1785 in the XXX year of his age. He was born in New Brunswick and received honors of the college at Princeton in N. Jersey. This monument is erected to his memory by his affectionate brother TLV."

Rosannah Millen was born in Pennsylvania around 1752; John, her husband, was born in Scotland around 1756. It is unknown when John came to America, when they were wed, or when they came to Georgia. Death records do indicate that John was a tanner and shoemaker. Rosannah died in 1810 from "inflammation of the stomach accompanied by pleurisy" which is inflammation in the lungs. John died of "paralytic affection."

"In memory of Julia Ann, Consort of Captain J. Cooper, who died on the 23rd November 1813 in the 25th year of her age. Also of William Cooper aged one year and 6 months. The just are happy."

This grave is shared by siblings Margaret and Francis Cole. Margaret died on December 14, 1848, when she was five; Francis died on the 31st when he was three. Margaret died from "convulsions"" and Francis died from an "ulcerated sore throat."

It is hard to see what island John Oliver is said to be from, but death records have him as being a native of Spain. Though he was from Spain, he was listed as being a resident of Savannah at the time of his death. He died in the summer of 1836 from consumption.

Many graves in this cemetery belong to more than one person; this one belongs to three. The epitaph reads:

> Sacred to the memory of Onesime Legriel, who was born at St. Marc in the Island of St. Domingo, December 29th, 1802 and departed this life March 5th 1840 aged 38 years and 2 months. A loving husband, an affectionate father, a sincere friend and a truly honest man. Also to the memory of Nerestan Legriel who was born at Port Au Prince in the Island of St. Domingo, January 6th 1799 and departed this life January 16, 1838 aged 39 years. Also to the memory of Charles Perony De Istria who was born at Ajacio in the Island of Corsica, Aug 6th 1764 and departed this life January 13th 1826 aged 62 years and 5 months. "Blessed are the dead who die in the Lord."

When I first saw Ann Caroline Cooper's grave (referred to in the records as Caroline), I thought that it was a tablet. Looking at it more closely while I was trying to remove the anthills, I saw that it was broken at the base. This feels like an overall representation of the tragedy that was the Cooper family's legacy, with a mother that outlived all her children.

When she was born in July 1818 to parents Ephraim and Lydia, Caroline was the youngest of seven children. Sadly, she did not get to meet three of her brothers as they died before she was born. John and Ephraim Jr. died in 1811; Ephraim died in August

Above left: "In memory of Capt. John Oliver, who departed this life 22 July 1836 in the 57th year of his age. A native of the Island of..."

Above right: The standing grave belongs to James and Elizabeth Shaw; James died in 1804, and Elizabeth died six years later. The tablet belongs to siblings Mary Louisa Matilda and William Lathrop; Mary died when she was one and a half while William died when he was only eight months.

Right: Onesime Legriel, Nerestan Legriel, and Charles Perony De Istria are buried here together.

of fever at age two, and John died in September of worm fever just shy of his fourth birthday. Joseph died in 1814 from intermittent fever when he was three. All three Cooper boys are buried in Colonial Park as well, but unfortunately their tombstones have been lost to time and their graves are unmarked. They lost their patriarch, Ephraim Sr., in 1825 to dropsy, which is swelling from heart failure or kidney disease. Caroline died on September 2, 1828, at ten years old from fever. In 1839, Lydia lost two more of her children; Thomas in January from spasms at age twenty-nine, and Sarah in September at age twenty-three from fever. Julia lived until 1865, dying from paralysis when she was fifty. Lydia lived another eight years, dying in 1873 from pneumonia when she was eighty-three years old.

Mary Ann was born to Pierre and Rebecca Douville on January 19, 1806. She was the oldest of three children and the only one to survive to adulthood; she was three when her brother died and eight when her sister died. She married Moses Coburn on March 22, 1829, in Providence before they later settled in Savannah. They had three children together, all of which were born in Savannah: Moses in 1834, Helen in 1836, and Wiliam in 1838. Sadly, Mary Ann would die on August 27, 1841, during childbirth with her fourth child. Most death records indicate a stillbirth during this time. With no record of a child being born and no stillbirth in the record, it seems likely that Mary Ann needed a c-section and could not get one; she was therefore unable to deliver.

Above left: "Ann Caroline, daughter of Ephrium & Lidia Cooper died on the 1st of Sept 1828 aged 10 years and 2 months."

Above right: This is the grave of Thomas Cooper, the brother of Ann Caroline. He was a physician living in South Carolina; he died at age twenty-nine in 1839 from "spasms."

"Sacred to the memory of Mary Ann, wife of Moses Coburn and daughter of Capt. Peter and Rebecca Douville. She was born in Providence, RI January 10, 1806 and died in Savannah August 27, 1841 aged 35 years, 7 months and 8 days."

The grave of Grace and James Belcher always stood out to me because of the little daisies that are carved into the top of it. Grace Belcher was born Grace Hastings in England in 1748 per family tree records. She married William Carr around 1768 in England and they eventually came to Georgia; at that time, they had a daughter, Jane, in 1769. Sadly, William would pass away in 1770. It would be almost ten years before Grace remarried; she married James Belcher in 1788. They had a son, James Price Belcher, in April 1788; she would sadly lose her daughter, Jane, that same year. Though the records do not go back far enough to tell us why, Grace died on January 14, 1793, and her son, James, followed on February 21 of that same year.

Theodosius "Thad" Eaton was born in Massachusetts around 1785. He was a resident of Savannah when he died at age fifty-three from "inflammation of the brain." His occupation is listed as being a carriage trimmer. Trimmers primarily worked on ships, rearranging cargo and coal to keep the ship balanced; it stands to reason the same thing would apply to trains in the 1800s.

"In memory of Mrs. Grace Belcher wife of Mr. James Belcher who died Jan 14th 1793 aged 45 years. Also James Pryce Belcher son of the above parent who died Feby 21st 1793 aged 4 years and 10 mons."

Jane Achord was born to Lewis and Jane in Georgia in 1796. Lewis was initially with the Georgia Loyalists during the Revolutionary War but changed sides and served with the Patriots in 1782. She was the youngest of four siblings, with two brothers and one sister. Both of her parents died when she was just a teenager, with her father dying in 1809 and her mother in 1811.

She married John King, a tailor, on May 14, 1816. Before they were married, he had served in the War of 1812. They were married just over a year when Jane passed away. She died on October 4, 1817, when she was only twenty-one during childbirth with their first child; their baby was stillborn and buried with her. John remarried a woman named Sarah in 1818, but they never had any children.

Jane's epitaph reads:

> Sacred to the memory of Mrs. Jane King, consort of John R. King of this city, a native of Chatham County, Georgia, who together with her newborn infant departed this

"This stone is erected by Timo. Eaton of Boston Mass. in memory of his brother Thad. who died May 29, 1835 aged 51 years."

Jane King and her unnamed baby are buried here.

> transitory life October 4th, 1817, aged 21 years. Life is a race of mingled joy and pain, passion the spur and half blind the sense of rein; the steed is health, hopes glittering shades the prize that mocks our hearts but still allures our eyes right one we bound, and in false fortune trust anon comes death and lays us in the dust but earth may sink, the sun itself expire, still lives the soul; that spark of heavenly fire mounts to its kindred sphere when free from pain true friends on earth may meet and love again.

Frances Adams was born in South Carolina in 1808. She married J. A. LaRoche (James Archibald) on January 11, 1832. They had one child together, John, but he appears to have been stillborn in 1833. Frances would not live much longer, dying in November 1839 from "cancer of the left ovary."

This is the grave of the Warren family. Robert was born in Georgia in 1810 and was a clerk by trade. He married Sarah Pearce on June 11, 1829. They had two children together: Andrew in 1830 and Sarah in 1831. Tragically, they would lose both children within a few weeks of each other in 1833. Sarah died on September 24, 1833, when she was just a few months shy of her second birthday; her cause of death was whooping cough. About three weeks later, Andrew died when he was only three from inflammatory bowels. About six months later in April, Robert would die of fever when he was only twenty-four and was buried with his children.

Having lost everything, Sarah would eventually remarry a man named John Pearson in 1842 and they would have five children together; she is buried in Florida.

Above left: "In memory of Mrs. Frances S. Consort of JA LaRoche who died 4th Nov 1839 aged 31 years."

Above right: Serene Wise and Frances LaRoche are resting side by side in the southern part of the cemetery.

"Sacred to the memory of Robert B. Warren, who departed this life April 18th 1834, aged 24 years. Also, of his son Andrew J, who died October 14th 1833, aged 3 years & 5 months. And of his daughter Sarah, who died Sept 24th 1833, aged 21 months."

This is the grave of brothers James and John Crawford. John died in August 1832 when he was eight days old. James died in January 1834 when he was three years old.

"This stone is erected to the memory of Captain Joseph Trowbridge of New Haven, Connecticut, a citizen much respected for probity and integrity. He sustained a long decline of health with a calmness and resignation, having maintained a reverence for the principles and maxims of the Christian religion. He died in a good hope of future happiness through the merits of the Redeemer. December 17, 1790. Died in the 55th year of his age."

"In memory of William Thomson, a native of Scotland, who died Oct 24th 1819 aged about 30 years." William Thomson was a bricklayer who died from "fever" in October 1819. Per death records, he was actually thirty-five years old.

James Butler was a little over a year old when he died in November 1837. His grave is just inside the front gate of the cemetery.

This tombstone in Colonial Park Cemetery is so small you just might miss it. This grave belongs to Caroline Shearer. She was born on January 21, 1832, to William and Eliza. She passed away on September 13, 1834, at age two. Her cause of death is listed as being "inflammation of the brain." While she is buried here, most of her family seems to be buried in Laurel Grove Cemetery.

This is the grave of Patrick Stanton, John Harvey, and Matthew Weitman. Patrick and John are father and son. Patrick married Naomi Gugle in 1817, dying three years later when he was thirty-two. Naomi then married Matthew in 1829, though he died in 1837 when he was forty-four. Naomi never remarried.

This grave belongs to Captain William Patterson. "A native of Philadelphia, born Feb 11th 1788, Died Aug 14th, 1812. It's this the shafts of death on all the high, the low, relentless fall, regardless who the next shall be, called to obey the stern decree. Yet 'twas not death the mandate gave, "twas he who died that he might save, the judge eternal calls to rest, and man obeys the high behest."

This is the grave of Sumner Moore, age twenty-two. Born in Massachusetts, Sumner was a stone worker who died from fever in October 1825.

This vault contains the remains of the Scarbrough family. On the left, you can read the epitaph for Lucy Scarbrough Sistare, who was twenty-eight when she died in 1840. Tragically, Lucy outlived all of her children. She had two infant sons die, one unnamed at five days and William in 1837 at fifteen days. Julia died in 1837 when she was four, and Julian died a few months before his mother at age one.

7
Unusual Stories

Strange and Stranger

While researching any cemetery, you are bound to come across some unusual stories and circumstances. These next few graves being shared all have something odd about them, whether that be the stones, the names on the graves, or something else entirely.

Trying to sort out the grave of the Holcombe brothers was a little confusing, given that they all have such similar initials. Here is what I was able to find. The Holcombe brothers were born to Henry and Frances Holcombe. Their father served during the Revolutionary War as a chaplain. Their mother "was the manager of the Chatham Female Asylum."

The placement of "months" on the tombstone is confusing. Online has it being part of H.'s age of "13 months," but looking at it, it looks like it is part of H. W.'s age as "4 months." It may actually be, in fact, for all three boys. All family trees for the Holcombe family include a William Henry (or W. H. as it is inscribed). His birth dates vary based on each tree; if he were to be twenty-one years old when he died in 1800, he would have been born in 1779. Their mother would have been only twelve years old. Different times aside, Henry and Frances did not marry until 1786, when William Henry would have supposedly been seven years old. Given that it was the 1700s, this seems extremely unlikely.

An issue of the Savannah, Georgia, *Gazette* in July 1800 reads, "DIED, in Savannah on the 22nd, infant, master William Henry Holcombe, the third son, and sixth child, of the rev. H. Holcombe, aged 21 months and 11 days." This means the "months" in the epitaph applies to W. H. It also seems to apply to H., the third grave listed. Records show a Henry Holcombe, son of Rev. Henry Holcombe, dying of "bilious remittent fever" when he was fifteen months old. The issue comes in here with dates. The tombstone says he died in September 1804; the death records indicate that he died November 1805. I think this might have been an entry error, though. I went through the film strip that this record is attached to and I found a few notations for "1805," but there is nothing for most of the pages. Maybe the records got mixed together or maybe the grave got altered as we have seen before. In any case, there was a Henry Holcombe who died at around thirteen months who was the son of Henry and Frances. The biggest mystery here is H. W. He only has one record of existence, which is this grave (and subsequently his find a grave page online). Family trees that include him only have the find a grave as a reference. There are no death records or newspapers that can be linked to him like the other boys. Was he four months or four years? We may never be able to tell.

When I originally came across this grave, I believed she was the sister of Ann Caroline who I previously mentioned. Caroline's sister was born in 1817 and died in 1839 of remittent fever on September 23. With the date discrepancies, though, I became uncertain. That, and Caroline's sister was born Sarah Jane Cooper; this grave shows that her married name was Sarah Jane Cooper as she was married to Peter Cooper. Could this be the same woman, who married someone with the same last name, and the tombstone and death records are nearly a month off for her date of death? Or are they two separate Sarah Janes, born the same year and dying the same year in Savannah about a month apart, one married and one single? This seems to be one of the mysteries of Colonial Park.

I had a difficult time researching this grave at first because I tried researching John Cunningham; there are no interment records for a John Cunningham in Colonial Park. Looking closely and lightening the photo revealed that the grave actually belongs to John William Waudin, John Cunningham's apprentice. I wonder what John Waudin's life was like, that his boss was the one to pay for his tomb.

Most of what I was able to find about John William Waudin came from his father's will. His father, also named John, left his estate to be divided equally between John Jr. and his sister, Mary, who seems to have gone by Polly. Family tree records show that their mother, Susannah, had already passed away in 1783. John Sr. passed away in 1787. Polly and John Jr. both passed away in 1794, though it is impossible to say who was older as John Jr.'s birth records and age are not available.

While the name of Matilda's husband is not on the tombstone for some reason, there is a Matilda Hart listed as being from Ireland that died on October 11, 1820, from "fever." Given that 1820 was one of the years of the yellow fever outbreak, it seems likely that this is the fever they are referring to. The difference in date could be her death date *versus* her burial date or it may have simply been wrong; after all, even Edgar Allan Poe's birthday is wrong on his grave.

Matilda would have been seven when her younger sister, Bridget, was born. I cannot find Bridget in the death records but, given that she died in August 1820, it seems very likely that she died of yellow fever as well.

Mary Ann Dillon is buried with the Gillespie sisters, though I have not been able to find any relation between them. Mary Ann died in October 1825. Her burial was on the 5th according to records, though they have her as being two years old when her tombstone states she was a little over a year and a half. Her cause of death is listed as being convulsions and, without any indication as to who her parents are, there's no way to tell if or how she's related to the Gillespie-Hart family.

The death records for Mary Langdon show her cause of death simply as "casualty." A casualty of what? I cannot be sure. There was not a war or battle going on at that time, which is what I typically think of when I hear "casualty." It could also have been an accident of some kind.

"WH, HW, H. Sons of H & F Holcombe. Died July 22, 1800 aged 21; Feb 9, 1804, 4 months; Sept 21 1804 13. Of such is the kingdom of heaven."

Beneath this tree rests Sarah Jane Cooper. Per her epitaph, she was the wife of Peter Cooper, was born in Baltimore, and died on August 26, 1839, when she was twenty-two years old.

"This stone is erected by John Cunningham of Savannah, merchant. To the memory of his late apprentice John William Waudin, who died much regretted by him the 25th September 1794."

"Sacred to the memory of Bridget Gillespie who departed this life August 10, 1820, aged 12 years. And of her sister Matilda, wife of ... who departed this life October 15th 1820 aged 19 years; native of Parish of Killesnill, County Leitrim, Ireland. Also of Mary Ann Dillon, who departed this life October 5th, 1825 aged 1 year and 9 months."

"Sacred to the memory of Mary Langton who was born in Long Island, state of New York and departed this life March 11, 1819. This stone is erected by Levi James."

I am also not sure who Levi James was to her; if it were her husband, she would be listed as Mary James. It may be her brother or her father, but there are no records to show this.

There is not much out there on Thomas Langston, though his cause of death is listed as being from consumption on January 24, 1824. He is also noted as being a "non-resident," so he was not from Savannah. A newspaper article from 1821 lists him as being a freshman at the University of Georgia and that he was from Oglethorpe, which is closer to central Georgia. I cannot say what he was doing in Savannah at the time of his death. What is most striking to me about his grave is the fact that, of all the spots in the cemetery, they decided this would be the best spot to place a bench. Yes, directly over the grave of a twenty-one-year-old that died of tuberculosis is a park bench.

Theodora Ash is a prime example of being able to learn so much just by taking notice of a grave, which in this case is very intricately carved. There are poppies along the sides and a carving of a young woman with a scythe to symbolize her dying so young.

Theodora was born in South Carolina in 1753 to Cato and Sarah; it appears that she went by the nickname Dory. She was the oldest of three in her parents' marriage and then, when her mother remarried, she gained three half-brothers. All of the siblings were born in South Carolina, and it appears they lived in Colleton County, between Savannah and Charleston.

"Thomas J. Langston Departed this life January 1st, 1824 Age 21 years. Child of mortality here pause and think of death."

Backing away from Thomas's grave shows you have to lean on the bench to read it.

Here is a profile of the bench over Thomas's grave.

Her father died when she was four years old, leaving her uncle as executor of his estate. Her uncle, Joseph Ash, did not comply with his brother's wishes, depriving his three children of their inheritance. It took Sarah and the children's stepfather, Henry Livingston, to make a claim on their behalf. The uncle never appeared in court over the accusations and was therefore excommunicated from the church.

Sadly, in 1765, Dory would lose her stepfather as well; he had been in her life since she was five. Her mother remarried Charles Odingsell in 1766 when she was about thirteen. It looks like Charles was from Georgia as he was born in Darien, so this may be why the family temporarily relocated. Dory died on February 17, 1770, at age seventeen from an unknown cause in Savannah where she is buried. Her stepfather, Charles, died nine months later on Skidaway Island. The family appears to have gone back to South Carolina as that is where they are all buried.

Dory's story does not end here, though. While in Colonial Park, you can visit her grave which is just inside the main gate on the right-hand side of the path. You can also see her footstone which has her name and 1770 carved into it, but it is not where you would expect. Start at Dory's grave and head towards the eastern wall. Take approximately 110 steps (careful where you step!) and you will come to a line of vaults. If you look behind the vault on the far left, you will spot her footstone.

Why is it there? It is hard to say, though it likely stems from the cemetery being used as a camp during the Civil War. It could have to do with someone who, rather than change the age on her grave like other tombstones, thought it would be funny to move her footstone so far from the headstone. It also could have been that it was knocked over during that time and by the time it was found it was just stuck somewhere. It is unlikely that whoever did it was thinking of the teenage Dory buried here, who lost so much in her short life.

"Here lyeth the body of Theodora Ash who departed this life February 17, 1770 aged 17 years. If innocence or virtue could save a living mortal from the grave, Theodora thou had'n never died."

This is the footstone of Theodora Ash.

Theodora's headstone is located near the main gate of the cemetery. Her footstone is located behind the family vault to the left in this picture, near the gate on East Oglethorpe Ave.

Buried here are Sarah Harris Ash (daughter), Sarah Ash (mother), and John Ash (father). John died in 1822 when he was twenty-nine, Sarah Harris in 1834 when she was thirteen, and Sarah in 1836 when she was forty-five. While they are buried near Theodora's footstone, I have not found a relation yet.

Two stones randomly sit behind this family vault; the one on the right appears to be a footstone as it only has the initials. Like Theodora, these probably are not in the right place.

Bibliography

Family tree sources provided by findagrave.com, ancestry.com, Family Tree app, and Geneanet community trees index

Berinato, C., "That's so Savannah: How Many Yellow Fever Victims Are Buried in Colonial Park Cemetery?" *Savannah Morning News*, August 4, 2021, www.savannahnow.com/story/lifestyle/2021/08/04/savannah-history-cemeteries-colonial-park-yellow-fever-deaths-graves/5476392001/. Accessed May 22, 2024

Berry, S., and Barnett, T. L., "The Graveyard of Old Diseases | CSI: Dixie," *Csidixie.org*, May 7, 2019, csidixie.org/numbers/mortality-census/graveyard-old-diseases

"Colonial Park Cemetery | Savannah, GA - Official Website," *Www.savannahga.gov*, www.savannahga.gov/879/Colonial-Park-Cemetery. Accessed May 22, 2024

"Colonial Park Cemetery | Savannah, GA - Official Website," *Www.savannahga.gov*, www.savannahga.gov/879/Colonial-Park-Cemetery. Accessed May 22, 2024

"Colonial Park Cemetery, Savannah, GA - Burial Records," *Www.interment.net*, www.interment.net/data/us/ga/chatham/colonial-park-cemetery.htm. Accessed May 22, 2024

"Colonial Park Cemetery, Savannah, GA - Burial Records," *Www.interment.net*, www.interment.net/data/us/ga/chatham/colonial-park-cemetery.htm. Accessed May 22, 2024

Connecticut, U.S., Town Marriage Records, pre-1870 (Barbour Collection)

Georgia, U.S., Compiled Marriages, 1754–1850

Georgia, U.S., Marriage Records from Select Counties, 1828–1978

Georgia, U.S., Wills and Probate Records, 1742–1992

Index to Compiled Service Records of Volunteer Soldiers Who Served During the War of 1812

Loyalists in the Southern Campaign of the Revolutionary War, Vol. 1, U.S.

Marriage Records from Select Counties, 1828–1978

Michaels, T.C., and B., "The Tragic Dead in Colonial Park Cemetery," *GENTEEL & BARD*, November 21, 2022, genteelandbard.com/savannah-ghost-stories/2018/11/7/the-ghosts-of-colonial-park-cemetery. Accessed May 22, 2024

North America, Family Histories, 1500–2000

Revolutionary War Rolls, 1775–1783

Savannah Republican (Savannah, Ga.), 1824–1829, September 22, 1827, Image 3

Savannah, Georgia Vital Records, 1803–1966

Savannah, Georgia, U.S., Court Records, 1790–1934

Savannah, Georgia, U.S., Naturalization Records, 1790–1910

Savannah, Georgia, U.S., Select Board of Health and Health Department Records, 1824–1864, 1887–1896

"Some Medical Term Used in Old Records," *Www.mifamilyhistory.org*, www.mifamilyhistory.org/genhelp/diseases.aspx.

"That's so Savannah: How Many Yellow Fever Victims Are Buried in Colonial Park Cemetery?" *Savannah Morning News*, August 4, 2021, www.savannahnow.com/story/lifestyle/2021/08/04/savannah-history-cemeteries-colonial-park-yellow-fever-deaths-graves/5476392001/. Accessed May 22, 2024

The Georgia Journal (Milledgeville, Ga.) 1809–1847, November 27, 1821, Image 2

"The Graveyard of Old Diseases | CSI: Dixie," *Csidixie.org*, May 7, 2019, csidixie.org/numbers/mortality-census/graveyard-old-diseases

The South Carolina Historical and Genealogical Magazine, Vol. 22, No. 2 (April 1921), pp. 53-59

"The Tragic Dead in Colonial Park Cemetery," *GENTEEL & BARD*, November 21 2022, genteelandbard.com/savannah-ghost-stories/2018/11/7/the-ghosts-of-colonial-park-cemetery. Accessed May 22, 2024

U.S. Newspaper Extractions from the Northeast, 1704–1930

U.S., Atlantic Ports Arriving and Departing Passenger and Crew Lists, 1820–1959

U.S., Cemetery and Burial Records, 1852–1939

About the Author

Lexi has always had a love of all things dark and haunting, from true crime to ghost stories. It is no surprise that she fell in love with Savannah when she moved there nearly a decade ago. Savannah is, after all, one of the most haunted cities in America.

With a love for photography since she was young, Lexi has combined that with her love of spooky stories and travel for everyone to enjoy on her Instagram page, @octoberallyear_. She began fully embracing her interests after becoming a mom as she wants her children to follow their passions, even if it makes them "weird."